how are plants
helpful?

by Kelley MacAulay

🌳 **Crabtree Publishing Company**

www.crabtreebooks.com

Author
Kelley MacAulay

Publishing plan research and development
Reagan Miller, Crabtree Publishing Company

Editorial director
Kathy Middleton

Editors
Reagan Miller, Crystal Sikkens

Proofreader
Kelly McNiven

Notes to adults
Reagan Miller

Photo research
Crystal Sikkens

Design
Ken Wright

Production coordinator and prepress technician
Ken Wright

Print coordinator
Margaret Amy Salter

Photographs
Shutterstock: cover, pages 3, 5, 8, 9, 11 (left), 12, 13 (right), 14, 15,
   16, 17, 18, 20, 21, 24 (bamboo, fibers, medicine, recycle, vitamins)
Thinkstock: title page, pages 4, 6, 7, 10, 11 (right), 19, 22, 23,
   24 (carbon dioxide, oxygen, nature)
Wikimedia Commons: Alexcooper1: page 13 (left)

Library and Archives Canada Cataloguing in Publication

MacAulay, Kelley, author
    How are plants helpful? / Kelley MacAulay.

(Plants close-up)
Includes index.
Issued in print and electronic formats.
ISBN 978-0-7787-0002-9 (bound).--ISBN 978-0-7787-0018-0 (pbk.).--
ISBN 978-1-4271-9374-2 (pdf).--ISBN 978-1-4271-9370-4 (html)

    1. Plants--Juvenile literature. 2. Plants, Useful--Juvenile
literature. 3. Plant ecology--Juvenile literature. I. Title.
II. Series: Plants close-up

QK49.M23 2013   j580   C2013-904027-7
                                     C2013-904028-5

Library of Congress Cataloging-in-Publication Data

MacAulay, Kelley.
 How are plants helpful? / Kelley MacAulay.
     p. cm. -- (Plants close-up)
  Includes an index.
  ISBN 978-0-7787-0002-9 (reinforced library binding) -- ISBN 978-0-7787-0018-0
(pbk.) -- ISBN 978-1-4271-9374-2 (electronic pdf) -- ISBN 978-1-4271-9370-4
(electronic html)
 1. Plants--Juvenile literature. 2. Plants, Useful--Juvenile literature. I. Title.
II. Series: Plants close-up.

QK49.M17 2013
580--dc23
                                     2013023430

Crabtree Publishing Company

Printed in Hong Kong/092013/BK20130703

www.crabtreebooks.com   1-800-387-7650

Published in Canada
Crabtree Publishing
616 Welland Ave.
St. Catharines, Ontario
L2M 5V6

Published in the United States
Crabtree Publishing
PMB 59051
350 Fifth Avenue, 59th Floor
New York, New York 10118

Published in the United Kingdom
Crabtree Publishing
Maritime House
Basin Road North, Hove
BN41 1WR

Published in Australia
Crabtree Publishing
3 Charles Street
Coburg North
VIC 3058

Contents

Living things

People are living things. We need food, water, air, and shelter to stay alive. Shelter is what protects us from bad weather.

Plants are living things, too. Roots, stems, and leaves are parts of plants. Flowers and fruits are parts of plants that make seeds. Seeds grow into new plants.

seeds

leaves

flower

stem

roots

Natural resources

Plants are **natural resources**. Natural resources are things that come from nature that people can use to meet their needs. Animals, water, and soil are also natural resources.

We get many of the things we need to survive from plants and other parts of nature. We get food, shelter, and **medicine** from plants! Medicine helps us feel better when we are sick.

Plants provide food

Food gives living things energy to grow and move. Plants make their own food. They make food in their leaves using sunlight, air, and water.

All people and animals depend on plants for food. People eat plants. Animals eat plants, too. Some people and animals also eat the animals that eat plants.

Healthy foods

Plant foods are very healthy to eat. They provide people with energy and **vitamins**. Vitamins are things our bodies need in order to work properly.

wheat

spinach

We use different parts of plants for food. When you crunch on a carrot or bite into a beet, you are eating plant roots. Grains, such as wheat, are plant seeds. We use grains to make bread. You are loading up on leaves when you add lettuce and spinach to your salads!

Parts of homes

People use materials from plants to build their homes. Wood is a hard material from trees. Wood can be used to build walls and floors in houses. It can also be used to make tables and chairs.

In some places, houses are made of **bamboo** and other plants. Bamboo is a type of grass that has a hard, strong stem.

Natural fabrics

Did you know the clothes you are wearing could have come from plants? Cotton and other materials used for some clothing are made from plant **fibers**. Fibers are long strands of material. These fluffy fibers are growing on cotton plants.

Cotton is soft and strong. Jeans and socks are clothes made of cotton.

cotton plant

Plant medicines

People have used plants to make medicine for thousands of years. Berries from elderberry plants can be used to treat colds and flus. Ginger plants can treat upset stomachs.

ginger

elderberries

aloe vera plants

Some people put juice from aloe vera plants on cuts or sunburns. The juice can help skin heal. Plants can also make people sick, however. Do not use plants as medicine unless a doctor tells you it is safe.

Clean air

People and animals need to breathe **oxygen** to stay alive. Oxygen is a part of the air. We get oxygen from plants.

Plants take in a part of air that we do not use called **carbon dioxide**. They use this air, along with water and sunlight, to make food. After making food, plants send oxygen back into the air.

oxygen

sunlight

carbon dioxide

water

Plants all around

People use plants every day. Trees provide shade to keep people cool. Wood from trees is used to make paper. Wood can also be burned to heat homes or cook food.

sugarcane

maple syrup

Some of your favorite treats may come from plants. Sugar is made from a plant called sugarcane. Maple syrup and candy is made from a liquid found in maple trees.

Helping plants

Plants give us so much! It is important we do all we can to protect plants and other things in nature. You can help by creating less waste and garbage. One easy way to help is to bring your lunch to school in a lunch box instead of a paper or plastic bag.

Recycle paper when you are done with it. Something that is recycled is used again to make something new. Recycling paper saves trees from being cut down to make new paper.

Words to know

bamboo 13 **carbon dioxide** 19 **fibers** 14 **medicine** 7, 16–17

natural resources 6 **oxygen** 18 **recycle** 23 **vitamins** 10

Notes for adults and an activity

Help children "cultivate" a life-long respect for plants and other natural resources. Using a *Star Diagram, or other graphic organizer, invite readers to share what they learned about the different ways plants help people and other living things.

• Take a walk around your neighborhood. Encourage children to take notice of the different plant life around them, from grasses and bushes to flowers and trees.

• Be a Plant (and planet) Protector!

Use the information from this book and the resources listed here to learn how to protect and preserve plants and other natural resources. Help children create an online posting or use recycled paper to make a poster sharing their important message.

Learning more

Books

The ABCs of Plants (The ABCs of the Natural World) by Bobbie Kalman. Crabtree Publishing Company (2007)

Protect Nature (Environment Action!) by Kay Barnham. Crabtree Publishing Company (2007)

Websites

The Great Plant Escape: Children team up with Detective LePlant to identify plant parts and functions and explore how a plant grows.
http://urbanext.illinois.edu/gpe/index.cfm

*Free downloadable graphic organizers and other learning resources are available at www.crabtreebooks.com